for NEW BELIEVERS

LIFE-CHANGING WORDS OF FAITH
FOR EVERY DAY

HARRISON HOUSE
Tulsa, Oklahoma

12 11 10 09   10 9 8 7 6 5 4 3 2 1

Scripture Confessions for New Believers:
Life-Changing Words of Faith for Every Day
ISBN 13: 978-1-57794-949-7
ISBN 10: 1-57794-949-8
Copyright © 2008 by Megan Provance
P.O. Box 701403
Tulsa, Oklahoma 74170

Published by Harrison House, Inc.
P.O. Box 35035
Tulsa, Oklahoma 74153
www.harrisonhouse.com

CONTENTS

Introduction

Congratulations on accepting the Lord Jesus as your personal Savior! An awesome spiritual adventure awaits you. Your sins have been forgiven and all the mistakes and failures of your past have been forgotten by God. You have a new start, a clean slate. It's like you have been born again. In fact, that is exactly what has happened. Spiritually, you have been born again. You have been translated out of the dominion of darkness into the kingdom of light. The old man is dead and there is a new man living in you.

God's will for your life is victory, success, and dominion. He has promised you health, happiness, and abundance. Get in the Word and find out who you are and what God has promised you. But just because it's God's will for your life doesn't mean it will automatically happen. Everything we get from God, we get by faith. A key factor in releasing your faith is the words coming out of your mouth. There is power released in your life when you speak God's Word. It is a vital part of appropriating God's promises for your life. When you speak God's Word you are actually activating spiritual forces that will bring God's promises to manifestation in your life.

Jesus said in Mark 11:23, that whosoever shall *speak* to the mountain and say "Be thou removed, and be thou cast into the sea" and not doubt in his heart, but believe that those things which he *has said* shall come to pass; he shall have whatsoever he *saith*.

The confessions in this book are faith declarations based on God's Word. I encourage you to speak them daily over your life. No matter what kind of challenge you are going through, there is hope, there is help, and there is life-altering power in speaking God's Word. Be faithful to speak His Word. Say these confessions boldly, speaking with power and authority. Even if you don't feel like it, even if you are afraid, by faith speak the Word with confidence. Release your faith, lay claim to all the promises that are rightly yours. Now start speaking and get ready to experience the release of God's power in your life!

Start the Day with God

This is the day the Lord has made and I will rejoice and be glad in it. I make a conscious choice to let God's love, light, and life shine through me today. I am a child of God, and the Spirit of God lives in me. I am ready for anything and equal to anything because greater is He who is in me than he who is in the world.

God directs my steps today. I am spiritually keen, mentally alert, and physically strong. I am healed, healthy, and whole. I have a great attitude. I am determined to conduct my life in such a way that I will be a living witness to those around me. No matter what happens today, I know God will see me through.

Today is going to be a great day. Blessings of abundance, health, and favor are coming my way. I am confident, fearless, and courageous. I will fulfill God's plan and purpose for my life. I am on track, in step, and right on the mark concerning God's perfect will for me. I am not easily distracted but focused, disciplined, and committed to fulfill the destiny that God has for me.

Scriptures

This is the day which the LORD hath made; we will rejoice and be glad in it.

Psalm 118:24

It is of the LORD's mercies that we are not consumed, because his compassions fail not. They are new every morning: great is thy faithfulness.

Lamentations 3:22,23

In all thy ways acknowledge him, and he shall direct thy paths.

Proverbs 3:6

I can do all things through Christ which strengtheneth me.

Philippians 4:13

What shall we then say to these things? If God be for us, who can be against us?

Romans 8:31

I Have Been Reconciled to God

I have been reconciled to God through Jesus Christ my Savior. I am now in a favored position. Jesus came that I might have abundant life through His blood. He purchased my reconciliation. I am in agreement with God's will for my life. I am now in the family of God. God is now my heavenly Father. He chose me, He adopted me, He loved me so much He sent His Son to die for me to redeem me. I am no longer a servant but a child of God. He has given me His love, grace, and mercy. I am complete in Him.

My past is past; God has forgiven me and has pardoned me. Though my sins were once as scarlet, I am now white as snow. Through my union with Him I have the power to live a life of peace, a life of joy, and a life of victory. It's not by my works but through the shed blood of Jesus that I have been redeemed, restored, and reconciled to God.

Scriptures

"I have swept away your offenses like a cloud, your sins like the morning mist. Return to me, for I have redeemed you."

Isaiah 44:22 NIV

Now he has reconciled you by Christ's physical body through death to present you holy in his sight, without blemish and free from accusation.

Colossians 1:22 NIV

"Come now, let us reason together," says the LORD. "Though your sins are like scarlet, they shall be as white as snow; though they are red as crimson, they shall be like wool."

Isaiah 1:18 NIV

I Am Free from the Law of Sin and Death

The Spirit of Life has broken the chains of satanic bondage over my life. Satan no longer has control or influence in my life. The law of the Spirit of life in Christ Jesus has made me free from the law of sin and death. The Spirit of Life is now the dominating force in my life. The Holy Spirit empowers me, makes me strong, and gives me life. I now have strength, courage and spiritual authority to resist the devil and his influences.

I am no longer a slave to the devil. I am no longer bound or controlled by the forces of darkness; they have no hold on me. I am free from Satan and his bondages; I am free from sickness and disease. I am free from poverty and lack. I am free from worry and anxiety. I am free from death and destruction. I am free from fear and evil entanglements. I am free from depression and despair. I am free from sinful addictions. I am determined to live my life in complete and total freedom and victory. I am free in Christ Jesus and I am enjoying living free in Him

Scriptures

The law of the Spirit of life [which is] in Christ Jesus [the law of our new being] has freed me from the law of sin and death.

Romans 8:2 AMP

It is for freedom that Christ has set us free. Stand firm, then, and do not let yourselves be burdened again by a yoke of slavery.

Galatians 5:1 NIV

Where the Spirit of the Lord is, there is freedom.

2 Corinthians 3:17 NIV

I Am the Righteousness of God

Second Corinthians 5:21 says that we have been made the righteousness of God. Therefore, in obedience to God's Word, I boldly confess that I am the righteousness of God in Christ. This is not by my goodness, not because I am holy within myself but because, through the shed blood of Jesus my Savior, I have been made righteous and acceptable in the sight of my heavenly Father. To be righteous means to be in right standing with God. That's why I can go boldly into the throne room and obtain grace and mercy. I am righteous not because of what I have done but because of what Jesus has done for me. His righteousness is His gift to me.

Scriptures

For our sake He made Christ [virtually] to be sin Who knew no sin, so that in and through Him we might become [endued with, viewed as being in, and examples of] the righteousness of God [what we ought to be, approved and acceptable and in right relationship with Him, by His goodness].

2 Corinthians 5:21 AMP

As by one man's disobedience many were made sinners, so by the obedience of one shall many be made righteous.

Romans 5:19

Let us therefore come boldly unto the throne of grace, that we may obtain mercy, and find grace to help in time of need.

Hebrews 4:16

I Am Chosen of God

I am chosen of God, I am part of His chosen generation. I am a peculiar person, set apart for God's causes and purpose. He has made me a part of His royal priesthood. He has called me out of darkness and now I live in His marvelous light because of what Jesus did. I have dominion and authority in the realm of the Spirit. Satan is under my feet. He has no power over me. Sickness and disease, poverty and lack have no authority over me. Through the power of the blood of Jesus I take my place as a prophet, priest, and king over all the affairs of my life.

Scriptures

Ye are a chosen generation, a royal priesthood, an holy nation, a peculiar people; that ye should shew forth the praises of him who hath called you out of darkness into his marvellous light.

1 Peter 2:9

To him who loves us and has freed us from our sins by his blood, and has made us to be a kingdom and priests to serve his God and Father—to him be glory and power for ever and ever! Amen.

Revelation 1:6 NIV

You were once darkness, but now you are light in the Lord. Live as children of light.

Ephesians 5:8 NIV

Nothing Can Separate Me From God's Love

God loved me so much that He sent His only Son Jesus to die for me. Jesus took my place. He took the burden and anguish of my sin so I wouldn't have to. He was my substitute. His love for me was the driving force that caused Him to endure the cross. He is merciful, kind, and forgiving. His love has no limits; He never condemns me but always reaches out to me. He loves me unconditionally. He is concerned about every aspect of my life.

God's love for me is greater than any sin I have committed, greater than any failure I have had. God's love for me is an unchangeable fact of this universe. Nothing I do, nothing people do, nothing the devil does can separate me from God's love. Not death, not life, not angels or principalities—nothing can separate me from His love. God's love for me is eternal. His love knows no boundaries; it never gives up believing in me or reaching out to me. His love comforts me, His love sustains me, and His love encourages my soul and restores my hope. God's love endures forever.

Scriptures

I am persuaded, that neither death, nor life, nor angels, nor principalities, nor powers, nor things present, nor things to come, nor height, nor depth, nor any other creature, shall be able to separate us from the love of God, which is in Christ Jesus our Lord.

Romans 8:38,39

"God so loved the world that he gave his one and only Son, that whoever believes in him shall not perish but have eternal life."

John 3:16 NIV

Give thanks to the LORD, for he is good; his love endures forever.

1 Chronicles 16:34 NIV

Being a Godly Person

I have God's wisdom and insight in all the matters of my life. I am determined to have God's character developed in me. I will allow God's love, life, and light to shine through me. I am in agreement with God's Word and I boldly confess that I am strong in the Lord and in the power of His might. I put a guard over my mouth so that I never criticize or condemn. I will never say or do anything that would erode another person's confidence or self-image.

I will walk in love and manifest the fruit of God's Spirit on a daily basis. I will be quick to listen and slow to speak. My friends will find a receptive and understanding heart in me.

By prayer and praise I will create an atmosphere of God's presence in my life. I am keen and sensitive to the voice of the Holy Spirit and I am quick to obey whatever He tells me to do.

I put God's Word as first priority in my life; it is the standard and cornerstone of all my decisions. The truth and principles of God's Word are my benchmarks for every decision. God's Word is my guiding light, providing guidance and direction. I will meditate on God's Word day and night and do my best to obey its instructions. I am determined to live a life that is honorable and pleasing to the Lord.

Scriptures

The fruit of the Spirit is love, joy, peace, longsuffering, gentleness, goodness, faith, meekness, temperance: against such there is no law.

Galatians 5:22,23

His delight is in the law of the LORD; and in his law doth he meditate day and night.

Psalm 1:2

With my whole heart have I sought thee: O let me not wander from thy commandments. Thy word have I hid in mine heart, that I might not sin against thee.

Psalm 119:10,11

Renewing My Mind

I dedicate myself to renewing my mind by reading, meditating, and speaking God's Word. It is my desire to keep my mind pure and clear from anything that would hurt or weaken me spiritually. I think on things that are pure, lovely, just, of a good report, virtuous and praiseworthy.

I choose to think about good things, and I refuse thoughts that are inappropriate. I cast down vain imaginations. I will not let doubt, worry, or fear pollute my mind. I will be quick to respond to wrong thoughts and desires by replacing them with proper thoughts and by speaking God's Word over my life.

I refuse to fill my mind with the poison of gossip, backbiting, and jealousy. I will guard and protect my mind by not watching, reading, or listening to anything that is detrimental to my spiritual growth. I make a quality decision to meditate on God's Word and to keep my mind pure and undefiled that I might be receptive to God's voice and ever ready to do His will

I consecrate my mind, my will, and my emotions to God for His service.

Scriptures

Be not conformed to this world: but be ye transformed by the renewing of your mind, that ye may prove what is that good, and acceptable, and perfect, will of God.

Romans 12:2

Finally, brethren, whatsoever things are true, whatsoever things are honest, whatsoever things are just, whatsoever things are pure, whatsoever things are lovely, whatsoever things are of good report; if there be any virtue, and if there be any praise, think on these things.

Philippians 4:8

[Cast] down imaginations, and every high thing that exalteth itself against the knowledge of God, and [bring] into captivity every thought to the obedience of Christ.

2 Corinthians 10:5

Hearing God's Voice

God's Word says I am His child and I know His voice. Therefore I proclaim that I know God's voice and I will not be deceived by the voice of the enemy. I am sensitive to the voice of the Holy Spirit and I am obedient to His instruction, direction, and guidance. I am tuned in to the Holy Spirit and I am quick to hear His still small voice. I am mindful not to do anything that grieves the Holy Spirit. I am diligent to spend time in prayer, fellowship, and worship with the Lord so that I continually keep myself in proper spiritual condition to hear His voice.

I seek His wisdom and counsel concerning all matters of my life. He is faithful to speak to me concerning changes or corrections I need to make. I am faithful to do everything He would have me to do. He speaks to me through His Word. As I study and meditate on the Scriptures, their life-giving force gives me spiritual strength. God's Word enlightens my spirit and illuminates my mind. My union with Him grows stronger every day as I grow in my ability to hear His voice clearly and accurately.

Scriptures

This thing commanded I them, saying, Obey my voice, and I will be your God, and ye shall be my people: and walk ye in all the ways that I have commanded you, that it may be well unto you.

Jeremiah 7:23

When he putteth forth his own sheep, he goeth before them, and the sheep follow him: for they know his voice. And a stranger will they not follow, but will flee from him: for they know not the voice of strangers.

John 10:4,5

My sheep hear my voice, and I know them, and they follow me.

John 10:27

So then faith cometh by hearing, and hearing by the word of God.

Romans 10:17

Speaking the Right Words

God's Word says that by my words I am justified and by my words I am condemned. I put a guard over my mouth. I choose to speak words of life, health, and healing. I choose to speak only words that are gracious and kind.

I will not speak evil of any person. I will not gossip or spread rumors. I will not speak words of death, destruction, or discouragement. I will be mindful to speak words that encourage, uplift, and inspire others. I refuse to criticize, condemn, or complain.

I refuse to give in to the temptation to speak before I think. I refuse to speak the wrong words when I am frustrated or angry. I choose to not be sarcastic, facetious, or condescending in my communication to others.

I put God's Word in my mouth, and I speak His promises over my life and the lives of others throughout the day. I am sensitive to the needs of others. I am quick to speak words of comfort, peace, and kindness to everyone I meet. My words bring hope, faith, and encouragement to all who hear them.

Scriptures

*By thy words thou shalt be justified,
and by thy words thou shalt be condemned.*

Matthew 12:37

*Put on therefore, as the elect of God,
holy and beloved, bowels of mercies, kindness,
humbleness of mind, meekness, longsuffering;
forbearing one another, and forgiving one
another, if any man have a quarrel against any:
even as Christ forgave you, so also do ye.
And above all these things put on charity,
which is the bond of perfectness.*

Colossians 3:12-14

*Let no corrupt communication proceed
out of your mouth, but that which is good to
the use of edifying, that it may minister grace
unto the hearers.*

Ephesians 4:29

Psalm 23

The Lord is my shepherd, my keeper, my protector. He watches over me. He cares about every little thing that affects my life. I shall not want or lack for anything. He gives me rest and peace in my life even in the middle of a world of turmoil. He refreshes and restores my life. He is a breath of fresh air to my soul. He is my guide in my new life of righteousness.

Even though I may walk through a dark valley and feel like death is all around me, I will not fear or be in despair for God is with me. He said He would never leave or forsake me. His love and protection surround my life like a shield. He will allow no harm or evil to befall me. His strength and guidance sustain me in troubled times.

God is always blessing me and giving me good things. God blesses me so much that it makes my enemies jealous. His goodness, mercy, and loving-kindness will follow me all the days of my life. My daily quest is to live in His presence.

Scriptures

The LORD is my strength and my shield; my heart trusts in him, and I am helped.

Psalm 28:7 NIV

He satisfies the thirsty and fills the hungry with good things.

Psalm 107:9 NIV

Surely goodness and mercy shall follow me all the days of my life: and I will dwell in the house of the LORD for ever.

Psalm 23:6

End the Day with God

I am thankful for another day. I refuse to worry or carry any burdens concerning the activities of this day. I cast all my cares on my heavenly Father. I put all the events of this day behind me and refuse to be fearful or be anxious about anything I did or didn't do today.

I ask God to forgive me for any sin I may have committed today. I receive God's forgiveness and extend my forgiveness to anyone who may have offended me today.

God's grace is sufficient for every area of my life. His presence fills my soul. He is my refuge, my fortress, and my strong tower.

I choose not to be fearful concerning tomorrow. I put my future, my hopes, and my dreams in God's hands. I trust Him to fulfill His plans and purposes in my life. He will sustain me, He will uphold me, He will deliver me from all my enemies. God's supernatural peace refreshes and restores my soul.

God gives me sweet sleep. I will get a good night's sleep and wake up refreshed and revitalized, ready for a new day.

Scriptures

[Cast] all your care upon him; for he careth for you.

1 Peter 5:7

It is of the LORD's mercies that we are not consumed, because his compassions fail not. They are new every morning: great is thy faithfulness.

Lamentations 3:22,23

I will lie down and sleep in peace, for you alone, O LORD, make me dwell in safety.

Psalm 4:8 NIV

PRAYER OF SALVATION

God loves you—no matter who you are, no matter what your past. God loves you so much that He gave His one and only begotten Son for you. The Bible tells us that "...whoever believes in him shall not perish but have eternal life" (John 3:16 NIV). Jesus laid down His life and rose again so that we could spend eternity with Him in heaven and experience His absolute best on earth. If you would like to receive Jesus into your life, say the following prayer out loud and mean it from your heart:

> *Heavenly Father, I come to You admitting that I am a sinner. Right now, I choose to turn away from sin, and I ask You to cleanse me of all unrighteousness. I believe that Your Son, Jesus, died on the cross to take away my sins. I also believe that He rose again from the dead so that I might be forgiven of my sins and made righteous through faith in Him. I call upon the name of Jesus Christ to be the Savior and Lord of my life. Jesus, I choose to follow You and ask that You fill me with the power of the Holy Spirit. I declare that right now I am a child of God. I am free from sin and full of the righteousness of God. I am saved in Jesus' name. Amen.*

If you prayed this prayer to receive Jesus Christ as your Savior for the first time, please contact us on the Web at **www.harrisonhouse.com** to receive a free book.

Or you may write to us at

Harrison House
P.O. Box 35035 •Tulsa, Oklahoma 74153

OTHER BOOKS AVAILABLE
IN THE SCRIPTURE
CONFESSIONS SERIES

Scripture Confessions
Gift Collection (Leather)

Scripture Confessions
For Healing

Scripture Confessions
For Finances

Scripture Confessions
For Victorious Living

Scripture Confessions
For Moms

Scripture Confessions
For Dads

Scripture Confessions
For Kids

Scripture Confessions
For Teens

Available at bookstores everywhere or visit
www.harrisonhouse.com.

A Beautiful Gift Edition to Set
Life's Course for Victory!

Scripture Confessions
Gift Collection
3-¾" x 5-½"
Bonded Leather
ISBN-13:
978-1-57794-916-9

God has given powerful promises in His Word—
peace, joy, health, provision, and more. Let these
promises become reality for you, a friend, or a
loved one by agreeing with God's Word!

The *Scripture Confessions Gift Collection*
includes five books complete in one volume:
Victorious Living, Healing, Finances, for Moms,
and *for Dads.* This life-changing gift in beautiful
Italian leather is a convenient and powerful
Scripture resource designed to bring God's Word
into busy lifestyles.

Available at fine bookstores everywhere or visit
www.harrisonhouse.com.